COLLEGE LONDON PRESS

GRADE

04

SINGING

Songs & Teaching Notes for
Trinity College London
Exams 2018–2021

Includes CD of
piano accompaniments
and pronunciation guides

Published by
Trinity College London Press
trinitycollege.com

Registered in England
Company no. 09726123

Copyright © 2017 Trinity College London Press
First impression, September 2017

Unauthorised photocopying is illegal
No part of this publication may be copied or reproduced in any
form or by any means without the prior permission of the publisher.

Printed in England by Caligraving Ltd.

CW00506254

The Leprehaun

Trad.

arr. Joyce

(1827–1914)

Copyright © 1935 by Boosey & Hawkes Music Publishers Ltd.

Reproduced by permission from *Irish Country Songs Highlights* (ISMN 979-0-060-09806-2)

ham-mered and sang with ti - ny voice, And drank his moun - tain dew... And___ I laughed to think he was caught at last: But the fai - ry was laugh - ing too!___ As___ quick as thought I seized the elf; 'Your fai - ry purse.' I cried,___ 'The

The Lark in the Clear Air

Sir Samuel Ferguson

Trad.
arr. Tate
(1911–1987)

Copyright © 2017 Trinity College London Press

day. For a ten - der beam - ing___ smile to my

hope___ has___ been___ grant - ed, And to - mor - row she___ shall___

hear all___ my fond___ heart would___ say.

2. I shall tell her all___ my___

love,   all__ my soul's__ a - dor - a - tion   And I think__ she will__ hear   and__ will not say me__ nay.   It is this   that gives my__ soul   all its joy - ous__ e - la - tion,   As I hear the sweet lark__ sing   in__ the clear__ air of the day._____

Jeune fillette

Young woman, make good use of your time, as violets are gathered only in the spring.

This flower blooms for only a short time. All beautiful things are fleeting, and so are courtships.

In your fine age, take a suitor, if he is unfaithful, set him free.

Trad.
arr. Weckerlin
(1821-1910)

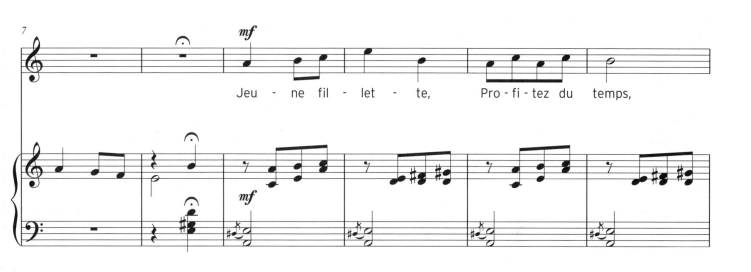

Jeu - ne fil - let - te, Pro - fi - tez du temps,

La vi - o - let - te Se cueille au prin - temps.___ La la la ri - ret - te,

Copyright © 2017 Trinity College London Press

La_ ri__ lon_ lan_ la,_____ La la la ri - ret - te, La_ ri__ lon_ lan_ la.

Cet - te fleu - ret - te Passe en peu de temps, Toute a - mou -

- ret - te Passe é - ga - le - ment. Jeu - ne fil - let - te,

Pro - fi - tez du temps, La vi - o - let - te Se cueille au prin -

Pro - fi - tez du temps, La vi - o - let - te Se cueille au prin -

-temps._____ La la la ri - ret - te, La__ ri__ lon__ lan__

la,_____ La la la ri - ret - te, La__ ri__ lon__ lan__ la.

Moreton Bay

Trad.
arr. O'Leary
(b. 1961)

One Sun-day morn - ing as I went walk - ing, by Bris-bane wa - ters I chanced to stray, I heard a con - vict his fate be-wail - ing, as on the sun - ny riv - er bank he lay. I am a na - tive of Er - in's is - land and ban-ished now from my na-tive shore, they tore me from my__ ag - ed par - ents and

Copyright © Mark O'Leary Music Publications 2004. All rights reserved. International copyright secured

from the maid-en whom I do a-dore. I've been a pris' - ner at

Port Mac-qua - rie, at Nor-folk Is - land and E-mu Plains, At Cas-tle Hill and

cursed Toon-gab - bie, At all those set - tle-ments I've worked in chains. But of all pla - ces of

con-dem-na - tion and pe-nal sta - tions of New South Wales, to More-ton Bay I have

found no equ - al, ex - cess - ive ty - ran - ny each day pre - vails.

For three long years we were beast-ly treat - ed and hea - vy irons on our

legs we wore; Our backs with flog - ging were cut to pie - ces and oft - en paint - ed with our

crim-son gore. And ma-ny a man from down-right star-va - tion lies mould-'ring now un-der-

-neath the clay; The Cap-tain Lo - gan he had us mang - led up - on the tri-ang-les of

More-ton Bay. Like the Eg-yp - tians and an-cient He - brews we

were op-pressed un-der Lo-gan's yoke, 'Till a na-tive black ly-ing there in am - bush did

give our ty - rant his mor-tal stroke. My fel-low pris - 'ners be all e - la - ted, may

all such mon - sters their death so find! And when from bond - age we're lib - er - a - ted our

for - mer suf-fer-ings shall fade from mind. Shall fade from mind, shall fade from mind, shall

fade,_____ shall fade from mind.

O cessate di piagarmi

Oh cease to scourge me, oh let me die!
Cruel, ungrateful lights, more than ice and more than marble, cold and indifferent to my tortures.

More than a serpent, more than a snake, brutal and indifferent to my sighs,
arrogant eyes, blind and dignified, you can heal me, and rejoice in my sufferings.

Nicolò Minato
(1627–1698)

Alessandro Scarlatti
(1660–1725)

Copyright © 2017 Trinity College London Press

Schneeglöckchen

(Snowdrops)
op. 79 no. 27

Friedrich Rückert
(1788–1866)

Robert Schumann
(1810–1856)

This may be sung in German or English.

Copyright © 2017 Trinity College London Press

Jeannie with the Light Brown Hair

Words and music by
Stephen Foster
(1826-1864)

I dream of Jean-nie with the

light brown hair, Borne like a va - por on the sum-mer air; I

see her trip-ping where the bright streams play, Hap-py as the dai - sies that

Copyright © 1940 by Carl Fischer, Inc.

22   Reproduced by permission of Boosey & Hawkes Music Publishers Ltd. from *Songs of the Americas* (ISMN 979-0-060-09269-5)

dance on her way. Ma - ny were the wild notes her mer - ry voice would pour;

Ma - ny were the blithe birds that war - bled o'er. I dream of Jean-nie with the

light brown hair, Float-ing like a va - por on the soft sum-mer air.

The Man in the Moon

Jean Phillips

Eric H Thiman
(1900-1975)

Allegretto, ma con anima ♩. = *c.* **80**

Copyright © Chester Music Limited trading as J Curwen and Sons. All Rights Reserved.
International Copyright Secured. Used by permission of Chester Music Limited trading as J Curwen and Sons

Dinah's Song

Tom Rothfield

Esther Rofe
(1904-2000)

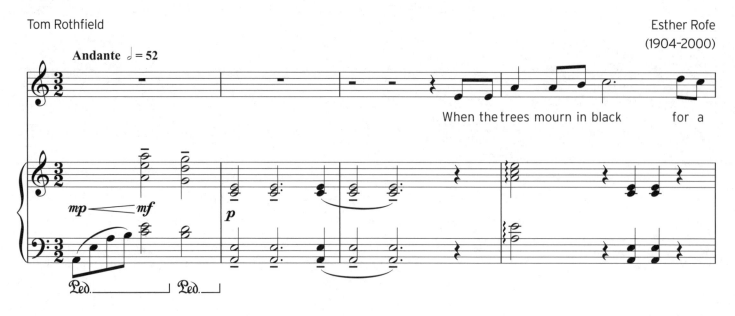

When the trees mourn in black   for a

day   long dead   Do I   see you there, weep-ing for   me?

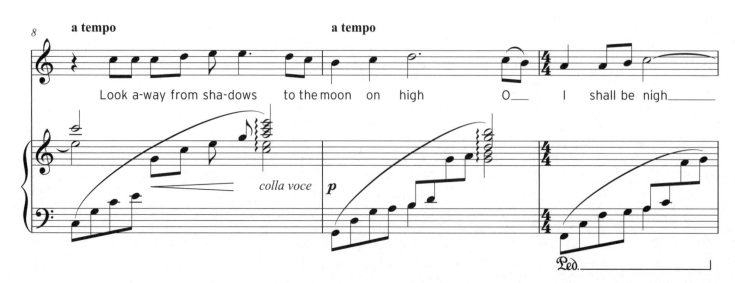

Look a-way from sha-dows   to the moon   on   high   O__   I   shall be nigh____

Copyright © All Music Publishing. All rights controlled and administered by Hal Leonard Australia Pty Ltd.
ABN 13 085 333 713 www.halleonard.com.au. Used By Permission. All Rights Reserved. Unauthorised Reproduction is Illegal

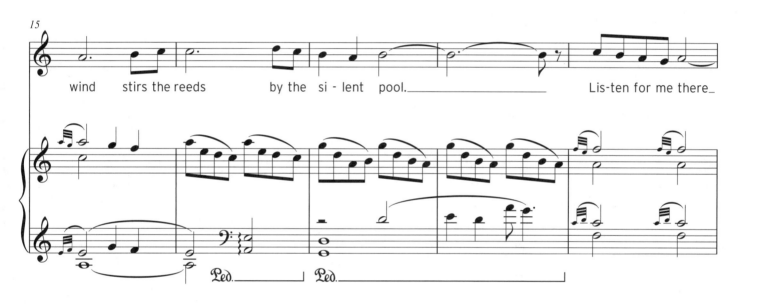

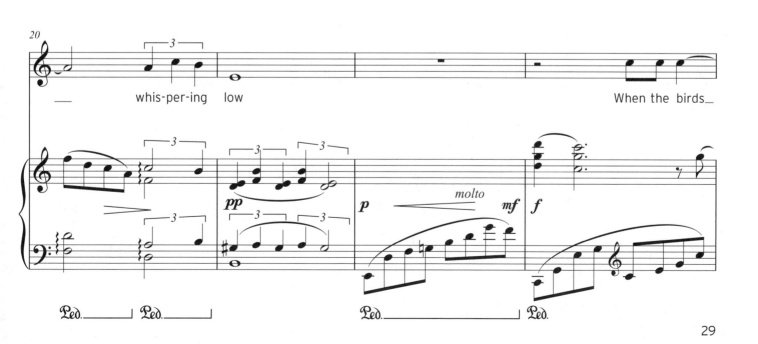

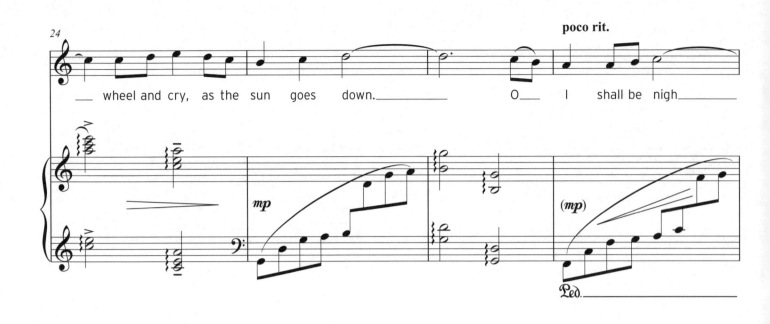

wheel and cry, as the sun goes down._____ O_____ I shall be nigh_____

com-fort your woe_____

Brighter (più anima)

In the bow-ing of trees_____ or the grace of a bird_____

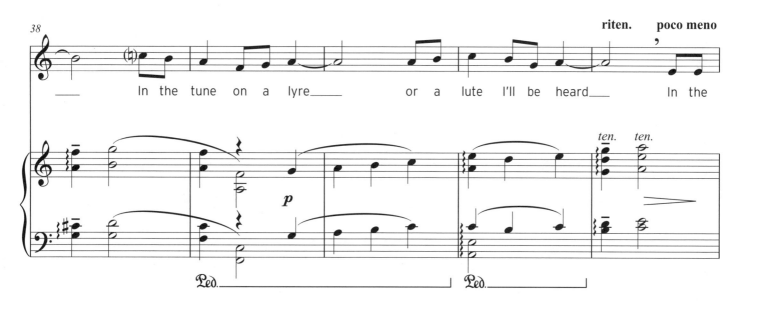

In the tune on a lyre___ or a lute I'll be heard___ In the

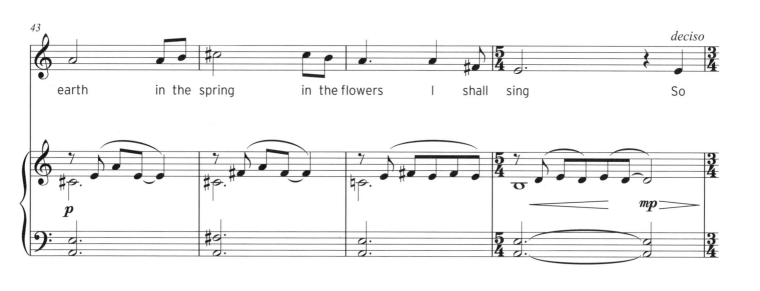

earth in the spring in the flowers I shall sing So

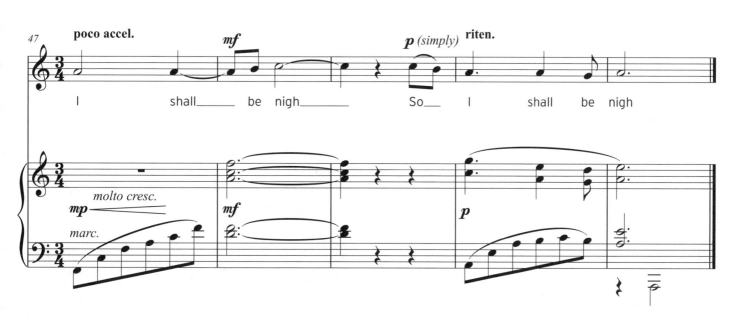

I shall___ be nigh___ So___ I shall be nigh

Shiny

James Reeves
(1909-1978)

Cecil Cope
(1909-2003)

Lyrics:
Shi - ny are the chest - nut leaves Be - fore they un - fold

The in - side of a but - ter - cup Is like po - lished gold.

© 1959, reassigned 1974 to Roberton Publications.
Reproduced by permission of Goodmusic Publishing Ltd., UK. www.goodmusicpublishing.co.uk

Career Paths

Garth Bardsley
(b. 1965)

Ben Parry
(b. 1965)

With a strong groove ♩ = 134

I should
like, one day,_ to be suc - cess - ful, I should like, one day,_ to be rich, But to a -
-void the jour - ney be - ing stress - ful, I am told by some you got - ta find your

Music © 2012 by Peters Edition Limited, London; Text © 2012 by Garth Bardsley

niche.* But which road should I choose at this junc - ture To make sure that my ta-lents I un - leash? I should hate at this point, my dreams, to punc - ture, So it is clear to me that one must find one's niche.** I could be a doc-tor or a sur-geon or per-haps a ra-di-o-lo-gist

*Pronounced 'nitch'
**Pronounced 'neesh'

which, I have to say, I am de - void.   I should

like, one day,__ to be suc - cess - ful,   I should like, one day,__ to find my

niche   'Twould be ea - sier if the list of jobs was less full   And I had

some i - dea of where, my voice, to pitch,   But I don't, and my thoughts are all in

*Optional bars 39–72 have been omitted.

Nine Lives

from *The Cat's Whiskers*

Words and music by
Peter Thorne
(b. 1955)

With a beat ♩ = 132

Nine   lives,   We've got   nine   lives   to   lead,___

Nine   lives,_____   And they're   fine   lives   in - deed.___

Copyright © Banks Music Publications 2002. Reproduced by permission.

fine lives in - deed.___ Two is the life spent out on the tiles, chas - ing our friends for miles and miles.__ We've got Nine lives, nine__ lives,__ nine lives to live.___ Nine lives, nine, nine, nine and we live them here and now,___

Nine lives, nine lives, We all get through some-how

When I re-mem-ber three, four and five it makes me so hap-py for

be - ing a - live. We got Nine lives, nine lives,

nine lives to live. Nine lives,

ni - ni - ni - ni - ni - ni - nine times a - live,___

Nine lives, nine___ lives, Fe - lines will sur - vive,___

Six, se - ven, eight and___ nine,___ This lit - tle pus - sy - cat's

gon - na be fine!__ Nine lives, nine__ lives,__ nine lives to live.

Teaching notes

Trad. *arr.* Joyce   The Leprehaun   page 2

Leprehauns, or leprechauns, are a type of Irish fairy, one of the 'little people' of folklore. They are usually depicted as being under a metre in height, bearded and dressed in green. Their trade is making and mending shoes but they all have a pot of gold, which is hidden at the end of a rainbow. Of an intelligent and devious nature, often being involved in all sorts of mischief, they will do anything to avoid being caught by humans for if they are caught they risk having to grant three wishes or losing their gold in return for their freedom. However, dealing with leprechauns is supposed to be a tricky business so even if one does get caught, he can usually find ways to escape without giving anything up.

That is certainly the case in this song. The narrator spies a leprechaun with his 'cruiskeen' or small drinking jug by his side and, believing that he can capture the fairy and win the 'purse of gold' he laughs. 'But the fairy was laughing too' means that very early in the song we know that things will not quite work out the way we might expect and indeed the leprechaun tricks the narrator into looking away and so manages to escape.

There is a moment of complete quiet before you begin to sing so don't be in a hurry to get started. Feel the pulse of the song right from the beginning, singing with plenty of energy but not rushing. Try emphasizing the consonants throughout as this will give a slight feeling of detachment to the words and also allow them to project well. Remember to slow down then speed up slightly before picking up to *Tempo I* in the final verse to communicate the trick the leprechaun plays. The accompaniment is quite sparse at times so you will need to practise singing this song slowly at first to ensure that all the notes are centred and in tune. Keep a feeling of laughter throughout the song with your eyes really lighting up.

There are all sorts of stories about fairies of one sort or another across the world. Can you find something out about any fairytales that are native to where you live?

Trad *arr.* Tate   The Lark in the Clear Air   page 6

This particular version of 'The Lark in the Clear Air' shows how a song can be shaped by many and diverse influences. The melody is from a traditional Irish air called 'An Trailluir'. It was then set with words by the 19th-century Irish poet, Sir Samuel Ferguson, whose wife was captivated by the tune. A visitor to the Fergusons' house - the Swedish harpist, Adolf Sjodern - was also enchanted by the tune and played it many times before the 20th-century English composer, Phyllis Tate, took and arranged the song with this piano accompaniment.

It is an ecstatic song of happiness as a young man plans to tell his loved one how he feels and how he hopes that she will feel the same. Although the main character in the song is traditionally a man, a female singer can deliver this song just as effectively, as the emotions of joy and hope are universal.

Although dealing with big emotions, the song remains quite delicate and you need to ensure that there is a lovely smooth *legato* line with the phrases well nourished by the breath. There are plenty of awkward English diphthongs, where two vowel sounds combine in a single syllable such as 'day', 'dear', and 'hear' so think carefully about how to sing these, especially on the longer held notes. The second verse has a broad dynamic range from *p* to *f* so experiment with these different colours, thinking how they enhance the communication of moods.

For many living in an urban environment, the sound of the 'sweet lark' can only be imagined. Try tracking down a recording of the bird song. There are many birds that sing or make distinctive sounds such as the cuckoo or the owl and composers have often tried to imitate their sounds in music. Can you find other songs about birds and their calls?

Trad. *arr.* Weckerlin Jeune fIllette   page 9

This song comes from the 18th century and is one of a number of popular rustic songs, called 'bergerettes' or 'shepherdesses' airs', researched by the composer Jean-Baptiste Weckerlin who wrote accompaniments to the tunes he collected.

The words of the song are quite forthright, telling the young lady to enjoy the time while she is young because time passes quickly and so does love. She needs to find a young man and not to worry if he is unfaithful as she can also be unfaithful in return! So the whole needs to be delivered with high spirits and vivacity, setting a tempo that allows for careful planning of the *rit.* at the ends of the two verses. These are very important as they allow you to communicate the wittiness of the words very effectively. Be prepared to 'kick off' again for the choruses and keep them moving, especially through the 'la la la rirette' passages which really suggest playfulness and laughter. Notice through these choruses how the dynamics change quite suddenly, starting *mf* then going down to *p* before a quick *crescendo* up to *f* with a drop back to *p* before finishing *f*. Think of how you can use your air flow and air pressure to help you achieve these almost abrupt contrasts, remembering not to constrict the throat or jaw, particularly on the quieter notes. On the note that is marked with a *crescendo*, you could add a *portamento*. This term comes from the Italian meaning 'carrying' and is a slide between two notes of different pitches. You could practise sliding between different notes, then adding in a *crescendo* to your slide to see how you can manage this effect before putting it into the song.

Do you think that this song would work with other instruments and not just the piano as an accompaniment? It so what instruments would you add? Could you write some rhythms or notes that other instruments could play?

Trad. *arr.* O'Leary   Moreton Bay   page 13

Moreton Bay is situated about 14 km from Brisbane on the eastern coast of Australia. It is a beautiful and scenic place, which attracts many visitors but it has a rather dark past and this song tells the tale of that history. In the early 19th century transportation was a common practice. This was a form of exile where petty criminals from the UK or Ireland were 'transported' to penal colonies in Australia to serve out their punishments. One of the most infamous of these colonies was in Moreton Bay under the notorious Captain Patrick Logan between the years 1825-1830. He was known for his particularly cruel treatment of prisoners, with many being kept in heavy chains, repeatedly flogged and also starved. The indigenous Aboriginal people were also in conflict with the settlers from Europe, including Logan and his soldiers, and he was killed by one of them in 1830, much to the relief of his prisoners.

The convict in this song is from Erin's island or Ireland and has been imprisoned in many places before coming to Moreton Bay. He talks of all the hardships and of being 'mangled up' on 'triangles', which were three wooden beams used to hold up the prisoners while they were being flogged. The melody is probably an Irish one, in keeping with the convict's nationality and it is quite a jolly tune in a major key. So you have to put across the horrors of the text with really clear diction and a keen understanding of the man's suffering or the meaning will be missed. Choose both your tempo and your dynamic range with great care and feel the change of mood at the close as the joyful thought of liberation emerges. As the note lengths increase at the end think about how you can communicate the idea that, with time, the painful memories will fade.

Do you think it is hard to sing a sad song that is written in a major key? Can you find any other songs that have a sad theme and use a major key? Or maybe a happy song that uses a minor key?

Scarlatti   O cessate di piagarmi   page 18

Alessandro Scarlatti was an Italian composer from the Baroque period. He was famous for his operas and chamber cantatas. This aria comes from his opera, *Il Pompeo*, composed when he was only 22 years old. In the opera, the character Sesto sings this to Issicratea, who he loves but she does not return his love being, in his eyes, 'fredde e sorde' or 'cold and deaf' to his sufferings.

Italian opera of the period often consisted of *recitatives*, which were written almost like speech and were used to advance the story and arias, such as this one, which were used to capture and express a character's emotions. So you need to sing this with a real sense of immersion in the feelings of rejection and despair experienced by Sesto. There are many repeated notes in the music and these give a feeling of emphasis, especially as they rise in pitch, highlighting and intensifying the emotion. You need to ensure that each repeated note is sung completely in tune with its neighbour, paying particular attention to how the sound will change as the vowel shapes alter.

Some performers will choose to sing the second verse, after the *ritornello*, or instrumental interlude, slightly slower than the first so you could consider this. You will also need to think of adding some ornamentation or embellishment to the second verse as this was common performance practice in the Baroque period where material was repeated. Make sure that anything you add is always fully integrated into the melody and does not become untidy or unrhythmic.

Try finding some recordings of this sung by different voices. See how they each make the aria their own by adding their own ornaments and other musical touches. How can you make your performance your own?

Schumann   Schneeglöckchen (Snowdrops)   page 20

Robert Schumann was perhaps one of the most influential composers of the Romantic era. He studied law before concentrating on becoming a concert pianist but an injury to his right hand meant that he had to give up that ambition. Instead he turned to composing, writing almost exclusively for the piano until 1840. He then shifted his attention to songs, which are almost a new form of song for the time in which the piano assumes an equal importance with the voice, adding another layer of communication to the whole.

Certainly in this song the piano plays a significant part in representing the sound of the bell that is made as the frozen snow hangs from the delicate stem of the snowdrop.

This continues through the song as the snowdrops ring in the coming of spring. To match the delicacy of the RH piano work, you should aim for a very focussed but light and graceful sound keeping the tempo of the song relaxed but not too slow. The metronome marking, which would have been added by Schumann himself, is a good guide to an appropriate speed. The three verses are almost identical but you need to think how to vary the tonal colours to suggest the excitement of looking forward to the arrival of spring in the final verse. You could try practising using one of the phrases from the song that is marked *p*, singing it a few times quietly but each time thinking of a different emotion. What does it feel like, and sound like, for example if you sing quietly and sadly, or quietly and happily, or even quietly and angrily? Not all emotions will be appropriate to this song but you could try and think of even more to experiment with.

Listen to some other songs by Schumann and think how he has used the piano accompaniment in these to suggest different moods.

Foster   Jeannie with the Light Brown Hair   page 22

Both the words and music of this song were written by the 19th-century American songwriter, Stephen Foster. He was a largely self-taught musician who wrote over 200 songs and he is sometimes credited with being one of the founders of American popular music. Certainly many of his simple yet effective melodies are still well known today.

It seems that this song was written to his wife Jane whose nickname was Jennie. Stephen's marriage to Jane was not an easy one and he wrote the song when they were living apart, possibly in an attempt to win her back. So there is a sense of longing in the 'dreaming' of Jeannie and the song needs to be sung with a real sense of her graceful beauty. Whilst there may be a feeling of simplicity and immediacy in both music and text, the relatively large vocal range of the song needs to be handled with care. Phrases move quickly over transition points in the voice, so thought needs to be given how to ensure even tone across the whole. Lower notes need to resonate without forcing and higher notes should be produced without strain. The whole needs to be sung very cleanly without any hint of sliding between notes so you could practise by working on individual bars with just a continuous 'zzz' sound, then one vowel sound to manage the larger intervals before finally putting in the words.

Are there other songs by Stephen Foster you could find to listen to or even learn to sing?

Thiman   The Man in the Moon   page 24

Eric Thiman, an English organist and composer, was largely self-taught but went on to achieve an FRCO and a MusD. He was a Professor of harmony at the Royal Academy of Music and the Dean of the Faculty of Music at London University.

The flowing compound triple metre here gives a feeling of the moon 'sailing along' and this song needs to be sung with animation and life. The longer held notes at the beginnings and in the middle of phrases could be 'warmed' through to give them directions and to keep a sense of forward momentum. Most phrases are easily sung in one breath but, in the second verse, think about taking a good breath after the word 'careful' so that you can sing through 'I didn't fall out of the moon' in one, with enough air to support a broad *crescendo* on the word 'fall'. Try practising long held notes at different pitches in your voice, keeping them steady before trying to add a well-graded *crescendo* on each one. Make sure that the phrase 'I think I'd be rather lonely though' is brought out well even though it is quiet by slowing the tempo and also using the *tenuto* markings to point the words.

Many people believe that they can see a face when looking at the moon but, across the world, there are also legends and stories about the man in the moon and how he got there. In the late 1960s Neil Armstrong became the first person actually to walk on the surface of the moon. What can you find out about that first lunar landing?

Esther Rofe was a 20th-century Australian musician and composer. After studies at the Royal College of Music in London, she returned to Australia and became known for her compositions for the ballet.

The words for this very evocative song are somewhat enigmatic. The implication may well be that the person in the song who is weeping is sad because a loved one has died. The song is ultimately one of consolation though as the spirit of the loved one continues to live on in the natural world and in the sounds of musical instruments, bringing comfort by being 'nigh' meaning near or nearby.

The song has a changing metre that moves from $\frac{3}{2}$ to $\frac{4}{4}$ to $\frac{3}{4}$ to $\frac{5}{4}$ then back to $\frac{3}{4}$ and you need to keep a constant feel of crochet equals crochet as you negotiate these changes. Keep a strong connection with a steady pulse. You may find that walking in time to the pulse or clapping the pulse as you sing helps with this. In the three main sections of the song, you will notice that the melodic material is very similar but you will need to keep counting very carefully as the rhythms do change. Be especially careful to count through the long held notes and to make sure that you are always coming in at exactly the right place. There is a brief moment near the end of the song where the music moves into a major key so be sure to feel this change and sing raised notes very brightly.

Why do you think that the composer might have used different metres in writing this song? What effect do you think that the few bars of a major key have near the end of the song?

Cecil Cope was a 20th-century English composer and teacher who sang as a chorister in Lichfield Cathedral before studying at the Royal Academy of Music and Trinity College in London, where he later taught singing.

The words to this song are very visual, describing first the shine of things in the daytime before evoking an image of the light cast by a winter moon. The chestnut tree referred to in the opening line is probably a sweet chestnut tree whose leaves are particularly glossy and the buttercup is a wild flower with highly lustrous yellow petals. A shilling is an old English coin first introduced in around 1500 and originally minted in silver. When new these coins were particularly shiny.

The structure of the music is in two sections matching the move in the poem from the day time to the night time. The first part is accompanied by a rippling piano part, which moves into block chords as the moon appears. This part should be sung more slowly as indicated by the instruction *meno mosso* but also *sostenuto* which means with a very smooth, sustained line. Think how to manage the breath pressure here, ensuring notes are held with an even tone and that each moves seamlessly into the next, especially over the large rising intervals of the octave and the sixth. The use of the sixth is a feature at the opening of the song too though here it is a descending sixth so be sure to pitch these intervals very carefully. Notice how the whole moves from some robust *mf* and *f* singing at first to an ethereal *pp* towards the close so use these dynamics to emphasise the contrasting images.

Painters are very influenced by the quality of light around them. Can you find any paintings that you think particularly capture a sense of light and shine? Or are there any that really manage to capture the atmosphere of the light of the moon?

Ben Parry is a British composer, arranger, conductor and singer. He studied at Cambridge University where he sang in the choir of King's College. He now works extensively with young musicians in his roles as director of the Junior Academy at the Royal Academy of Music in London and also as a director of the famous Eton Choral Courses for young singers.

This song is all about the words. It is almost in the tradition of a patter song, which is a fast, usually comic song where every syllable of text has one note and where the whole is delivered almost 'non-stop'. So you need to ensure that your diction is really clear. To help with your articulation, you could try practising some tongue twisters before you sing, such as 'six sticky skeletons' or 'if a dog chews shoes, whose shoes does he choose?' Try saying them out loud then set them to music. You could even make up your own tongue-twisting words.

Keep working on breathing quickly and efficiently too as there is often not much time to inhale deeply. You could cut the longer notes at ends of phrases slightly short to give yourself more time, remembering not to snatch breaths or to lift the shoulders but to keep working the lower body muscles, albeit quickly. Feel the groove of the song too with really neat cross rhythms. Take care with the different pronunciations of the word 'niche' too, perhaps emphasizing them to add to the humour of the song.

Can you find some examples of patter songs to listen to?

Peter Thorne studied music at Oxford University and he has a life-long love of jazz. He likes to combine jazz and classical elements in his compositions putting in unexpected twists to suggest a mood.

This song, which comes from a set of songs called *The Cat's Whiskers*, is full of jazzy elements with plenty of syncopation and chromatic writing in the piano. There is a gradual feel of 'build' through the whole song as the key changes four times, rising a semitone for each different verse. Plan these very well in your performance, listening very carefully to the piano, which leads the key changes as you finish one verse before starting on the next. Try practising some rising chromatic scale patterns, perhaps using the words 'nine lives' as you sing or make up your own exercises using different arrangements of semitones. Keep the drive and energy going through the whole song, feeling the beat of the music and keeping the cross rhythms tight but also being careful not to over sing in the *ff* passages. Think about how much slower you want to sing in the last verse at the words 'we pity you humans' and remember to save enough energy to accelerate back into the final 'big' finish with a strongly held last note.

There is an old English proverb that says that a cat has nine lives: 'For three he plays, for three he strays and for the last three he stays'. This could be where the idea that a cat has nine lives comes from or it could simply refer to the fact that in one life a cat will play and head out to hunt while young but will prefer to stay home as it gets older! However, cats are well known for their incredible dexterity and their ability to land on their feet even if jumping from a great height so maybe this suggests they can escape from dangerous situations more than once, perhaps even nine times.

Can you think of other attributes that different animals are supposed to have?